THE BIOGRAPHY OF JOHNNY DEPP

Table of Contents

INTRODUCTION

Johnny Depp is an entertainer known for depicting unusual characters in films like 'Tired Hollow,' Charlie and the Chocolate Factory, and the Privateers of the Caribbean establishment.

Who Is Johnny Depp?

Johnny Depp handled his most amazing authentic film job in Nightmare on Elm Street. He started concentrating on acting vigorously, the examples paying off in 1987 when he handled a job on the TV show 21 Jump Street. He has since become known for his readiness to take on more obscure jobs in movies like Edward Scissorhands, Sleepy Hollow and Alice in Wonderland, as well as his featuring endeavors in the enormous financial plan Pirates of the Caribbean films.

During the 2000s, Depp became one of the most fiscally productive film stars by playing Captain Jack Sparrow in the Walt Disney swashbuckler film series Pirates of the Caribbean. He got basic acclaim for Finding Neverland and proceeded with his monetarily fruitful coordinated effort with Tim Burton with the movies Charlie and the Chocolate Factory, Corpse Bride, and Sweeney Todd. In 2012, Depp was one of the world's greatest film stars and was recorded by the Guinness World Records as the world's most generously compensated entertainer, with an income of US$75 million. During the 2010s, Depp started delivering films through his organization, Infinitum Nihil, and framed the stone supergroup Hollywood Vampires with Alice Cooper and Joe Perry before featuring as Gellert Grindelwald in the Warner Bros.

Considered one of the best entertainers ever as far as film industry draw and acknowledgment, Johnny Depp has shaped a strong bond with moviegoers crossing different ages because of his capacity to completely retain himself into an arrangement of dynamic characters. The gifted entertainer's genuine story is loaded up with similarly significant exciting bends in the road at standard with the plots of a portion of the films he's featured in throughout his vocation. During his initial years, Depp had melodic yearnings; notwithstanding, it wasn't some time before he found the charm of the big screen. The adaptable entertainer arose out of his high schooler symbol days to make progress in a string film industry hits. His remarkable capacity to rejuvenate characters has included high-profile joint efforts with top chiefs and a rewarding relationship with the Disney group in the 'Privateers of the Caribbean series. While he has gained notoriety for knowing what moviegoers need. Depp also has an inclination to pick projects dependent more upon the test of the job than the potential for film industry achievement. He has figured out how to track down the perfect harmony between picking jobs for the genuine romance of becoming consumed in a person's reality to repeating comfortable jobs with reestablished excitement.

EARLY LIFE AND PARENTAGE

Johnny Depp was conceived, John Christopher Depp II, on June 9, 1963, in Owensboro, Kentucky, to guardians John and Betty Sue Depp. Kentucky is a home rule-class city in the province seat of Daviess County, Kentucky, United States. Depp's dad functioned as a structural architect, and his mom filled in as a server and homemaker. Been the most youthful of four youngsters, Depp was removed and a self-conceded crackpot.

Depp and his family moved much of the time to oblige his dad's work, at last arriving in Miramar, Florida, when Depp was 7 years of age. The family lived in a motel for nearly 12 months until his father got another profession. Depp loathed his new home and, by the age of 12, started smoking, exploring different avenues regarding drugs, and participating in self-hurt because of the pressure of family issues.

In 1978, when Depp was 15, his folks got separated. As the most youthful of four, it turned into Depp's responsibility to go to his dad's office and get the week after week kid support cash. The split caused a break between Depp and his dad, and his mom later wedded Robert Palmer, whom Depp has called "a motivation."

Depp's mom gave him a guitar when he was 12, and he started playing in different groups. He exited Miramar High School at 16 to turn into a stone performer. He endeavored to return to school fourteen days after the fact; however, the chief advised him to follow his fantasy about being a performer. Depp joined a carport band called the Kids. The gathering became sufficiently fruitful to open for the Talking Heads and the B-52s; however, they scarcely made a decent living. Depp lived for a really long time in a companion's '67 Chevy Impala.

After modest nearby progress of the band in Florida, the band moved to Los Angeles in quest for a record bargain, changing its name to Six Gun Method. Notwithstanding the band, Depp worked an assortment of unspecialized temp jobs, for example, in selling. In December 1983, Depp wedded cosmetics craftsman Lori Anne Allison, the sister of his band's bassist and vocalist. The Kids split up prior to marking a record bargain in 1984, and Depp started working together with the band Rock City Angels. He co-composed their tune "Mary," which showed up on their introduction to Geffen Records collection Young Man's Blues. Depp and Allison separated in 1985.

Depp is of principally English plunge, with some French, German, Irish, and West African parentage. His last name comes from a French Huguenot settler (Pierre Dieppe, who got comfortable in Virginia around 1700). He is additionally plunged from frontier political dissident Elizabeth Key Grinstead (1630-1665), little girl of English grower and individual from the Virginia House of Burgesses Thomas Key, and an oppressed person of color. In interviews in 2002 and 2011, Depp professed to have Native American lineage, saying: "I surmise I have some Native American someplace down the line. My astounding grandma was a lot Native American, and she might have grown up in Creek Indian or Cherokee. It appears to be legit coming from Kentucky, which is overflowing with Cherokee and Creek Indian". Depp's cases went under investigation when Indian Country Today composed that Depp had never asked about his legacy or been perceived as an individual from the Cherokee Nation. This prompted analysis from the Native American group, as Depp has no archived Native parentage, and Native people group pioneers think about him as "a non-Indian." Depp's decision to depict Tonto, a Native American person, in The Lone Ranger was condemned, alongside his decision to name his musical crew "Tonto's Giant Nuts." During the advancement of The Lone Ranger, Depp was taken on as a privileged child by LaDonna Harris, an individual from the Comanche Nation, making him a privileged individual from her family but not an individual from any clan. Basic reaction to his cases from the Native people group expanded after this, including mocking depictions of Depp by Native comics. Dior's promotion highlighting

Depp and Native American symbolism for the aroma "Sauvage" was pulled in 2019 due to being blamed for social allocation and bigotry.

VOCATION AS ACTOR

He started his vocation on the big screen in 1984 when he met Nicolas Cage, who persuaded him to take a stab at acting. His most memorable job was in the thriller "A Nightmare on Elm Street" coordinated by Wes Craven. In the film, he assumed the part of Glen Lantz, the beau of the hero.

In 1985, he made his presentation on TV when he assumed the part of Lionel Viland in the show series Lady Blue.

He likewise co-featured in the satire "Private Resort" and showed up in the short film "Fakers." Johnny Depp started to turn into a high school symbol in the last part of the 1980s, assuming the part of cop Tommy Hanson in the TV series "21 Jump Street," which started in 1987 and was finished in 1990.

In the year 1986, he was essential for the movie "Unit" coordinated by Oliver Stone, where he assumed the part of Gator Lerner, a fighter in the Vietnam War; the film won a few honors, among which an Oscar Award for best film. That year, he caused situations for the film "Thrashin" since he was terminated for conflicts with the maker. He was additionally crucial for the short film "R. P. G." in the job of Vinnie Dooler. In 1987, he partook in an episode of the "ABC Hotel" series where he assumed the part of Rob

Cameron and again assumed the part of Vince in "R. P. G. II."

In 1990, Depp was the hero of the parody "Churlish little child," where he assumed the part of Wade Walker. In that year, he was important for the element film "Edward Scissorhands," where he played a person with a similar name as the creation. Because of his brilliant exhibitions, he was named for the Golden Globe Award for the best entertainer in satire or melodic.

Somewhere in the range between 1991 and 1993, he assumed a few parts as a significant entertainer, among which the interest in the blood and gore flick "Freddy's Dead: The Final Nightmare" and assumed the part of Sam in the lighthearted comedy "Benny and Joon." In 1993 he additionally featured in the element films "The Dream of Arizona" and "Who does Gilbert Grape cherish?"

In 1994, he assumed the part of movie chief Ed Wood in the film of a similar name. Regardless of winning two Oscars and being a contender for three Golden Globes, the film had a low pay. Notwithstanding, pundits applauded the exhibition of Johnny Depp. He likewise featured in the movie "Cassanova DeMarco," where he played a youngster who was incapable of prevailing upon his cherished and attempted to end it all.

Later he assumed the part of William Blake in the western recorded clearly "Dead Man." He was additionally the star alongside Christopher Walken in the film "Nick of Time" by John Badham.

In 1997, he coordinated, delivered, composed, and featured in the film "The Brave." In that same year, he co-featured in the element film "Donnie Brasco," where he assumed the part of Joseph D. Pistone, where he worked with entertainers like Al Pacino and Michael Madsen.

In 1998, Depp was the hero of the dark parody "Dread and Loathing in Las Vegas," where he played a writer named Raoul Duke.

In 1999, he played Ichabod Crane in the component film "Drowsy Hollow." In that very year, he appeared in the episode of the sitcom "The Vicar of Dibley" on the BBC; He was also the hero of the film "The Ninth Gate," where he assumed the part of Dean Corso.

For the year 2000, he assumed the part of Roux in the heartfelt element movie "Chocolate," which was coordinated by Lasse Hallström; He likewise partook in the emotional movies "Before Night Falls" and "The Man Who Cried."

In 2001, he was the hero in "Blow," where he assumed the part of George Jung, an ex-convict and previous US drug dealer who was essential for the Medellin

Cartel. In that same year, he played the reviewer Frederick George Abberline in the film "From Hell."

In a little while, he featured in the film "Privateers of the Caribbean: The Curse of the Black Pearl," delivered in 2003, where he assumed the part of privateer Jack Sparrow, who became one of his most well-known characters. On account of his incredible acting in that film, he won an award from the Actors Guild for the best entertainer and was named for the Oscar Award in a similar classification. In 2004, Johnny Depp showed up in the film "Tracking down Neverland" (Discovering the Land of Neverland), where he played the essayist James Matthew Barrie. In that very year, the entertainer likewise showed up in the component film "The mysterious window," in the TV series "Head honcho," in the film "Ils se marièrent et eurent beaucoup d'enfants" and the film "The Libertine."

In 2005 he featured in the movies "Charlie and the Chocolate Factory" and "The Corpse Bride." In 2004, Johnny Depp likewise established the creation organization Infinitum Nihil to foster movies in which he filled in as an entertainer or potentially maker. Somewhere in the range between 2006 and 2007, he got back to the personality of Jack Sparrow in the spin-offs of "Privateers of the Caribbean: The Chest of the Dead Man" and At World's End, separately. In the wake of completing the third Pirates of the Caribbean film delivered in 2007, he played Benjamin Barker, otherwise called "Sweeney Todd," in the film "Sweeney Todd: The Demon Barber of Fleet Street." In 2008 he was named for the Oscars and won the Golden Globe Award for the presentation in "Sweeney Todd: The Demon Barber of Fleet Street." For the year 2009, he played John Dillinger in the film "Public Enemies." He likewise partook in the episode "SpongeBob versus The Big One" from the energized series SpongeBob; there, he gave voice to Jack Kahuna Laguna, a master who shows riding the primary person. In 2010, he was the hero close to Angelina Jolie in the film "The Tourist," where Johnny Depp played Frank Tupelo/Alexander Pearce, an educator scholastic. For his magnificent presentation, he won the Teen Choice Award and People's Choice Award for best entertainer and was designated for a Golden Globe Award for the best entertainer in a satire or melodic. In that very year, he represented the personality of Tarrant Hightopp in the film "Alice in Wonderland."

In 2011 his voice typified the personality of a chameleon in the energized film "Rango." In that year, he featured in the film "Privateers of the Caribbean: in puzzling tides." For the year 2012, he played Barnabas Collins in the film "Dull Shadows." Likewise, the entertainer appeared in the vivified series "Family Guy," remembering his personality Edward Scissorhands. In 2014, he partook in the Disney film "Into the Woods," where he played the character of

The Wolf. In that same year, he was the hero of the film "Amazing quality," where he addressed the person Will Caster. After a year, he played Whitey Bulger in the show "Dark Mass" coordinated by Scott Cooper.

On May 27, 2016, the film "Alice Through the Looking Glass" debuted, where Johnny Depp again played the Hatter. He assumed a minor part in the ghastliness satire "Yoga Hosers." In October of 2016, it was affirmed that he would be essential for the cast of the film Fantastic Animals and where to track down them. In 2017, the fifth piece of the Pirates of the Caribbean adventure named "Privateers of the Caribbean: Salazar's Revenge" debuted, where Johnny Deep played his notorious person, Captain Jack Sparrow.

INDIVIDUAL LIFE

A vast number of fans are watching the fresh insight into Johnny Depp's own life. His most memorable marriage with Laurie Ellison flopped in 1985.

With the development of ubiquity, the rundown of Hollywood star relations was added with new names. A ceaseless hunger for opportunity, a troublesome person, joined with Johnny's personality, didn't permit relations to keep going long. Depp had a relationship with Kate Moss, Sherilin Fenn, and Winona Ryder; however, nobody wedded him.

In 1998 Johnny Depp met a model, an entertainer, and a vocalist Vanessa Paradis. He experienced passionate feelings for Vanessa, and they even wedded. The couple moved to Vanessa's country in France, where they had two kids. The girl Lily-Rose Melody was brought into the world in spring 1999, and the child John Christopher in the spring of 2002.

For his significant other's collection, Johnny Depp composed a few tunes.

The kids satisfied this family, and the entertainer felt quiet and calm. Yet, in 2012 Depp and Paradis reported their separation. The justification for the split was called Johnny's accomplice in the film "The Rum Diary" Amber Heard, with whom he became companions in 2011. In February 2015, the darlings got hitched.

In May 2016, Heard petitioned for legal separation following 15 months of living with the Hollywood star. The last point in the marriage was set in January 2017. While the attorneys were tackling procedural issues, Johnny Depp went on a visit with his melodic gathering.

The separation procedures were clear and outrageous: Amber expressed that Johnny was deranged and desirous. However, Heard committed an unfortunate error: the entertainer petitioned for legal separation three days after the passing of Depp's mom. However, the picture of the young lady who broke the family, where two youngsters were growing up, didn't work. Then, at that point, Heard bet everything: she created a video with a scene of viciousness. The police denied Depp from going inside 100 yards to his significant other.

Depp's exes Laurie Ann Alison and Vanessa Paradis supported him and said their ex never laid his hand on them. His little girl Lily-Rose Depp likewise upheld her dad. She posted on Instagram an old family photograph where Dad helps the young lady to walk.

Toward the end, Heard suddenly dropped the charges of aggressive behavior at home and accepted $ 7 million as pay. In any case, having gotten the cash, the entertainer expressed that she would give them to a noble cause, and the entire sum would go to the assets that help the casualties of aggressive behavior at home.

Johnny Depp is generally keen on the kids' life. He adversely acknowledged the report about his girl's relationship with the separated from Ash Stymest. Youthful Lily Depp started dating Ash two years before her adulthood, which upset her folks.

In March, it became realized that Johnny Depp recorded to the court 87 recordings, wherein clearly Heard showed her viciousness toward him. She incited the fights and, surprisingly, lifted her hand at Johnny. Depp's legal advisors are confident that Amber was acting ahead of time when she lied about the reality that Johnny beat her.

MELODIC CAREER

Johnny Depp became intrigued by music by watching his cousins. At age 12, his mom gave him an electric guitar that he figured out how to play in a self-trained manner while paying attention to music. Johnny began playing in a few carport groups until his band out of appreciation for his better half of that time, Meredith. Over the 80s, he framed a band called Flame and played with the Belgian gathering The Kids. Because of financial issues, he needed to leave music briefly and started to commit himself entirely to acting, the craftsman said.

He played the acoustic guitar in the film "Chocolate" and took part in the "Érase Una Vez en México" soundtrack. Being a companion of Shane MacGowan of the gathering The Pogues, worked together in the principal solo collection of the arranger. He was additionally an individual from the "P" bunch. He also partook in video clasps, such as "Into the Great Wide Open" by Tom Petty and The Heartbreaker in "Creep" by Radiohead. He teamed up with vocalist Marilyn Manson on the melody "No doubt about it" and Paul McCartney's "Queenie Eye."

In 2015, alongside Alice Cooper and Joe Perry, he framed a hard rock supergroup called "Hollywood Vampires," in which he was the guitarist. On September 11 of that year, they delivered their most special collection, which included 2 melodies made by Johnny Depp. In September, he performed two times with the band at the Roxy Theater in Los Angeles and the Rock in Rio celebration in Brazil individually.

In June 2019, their second studio collection, Rise, was delivered, and it comprises, for the most, a unique material, including tunes composed by Depp. The collection additionally includes a cover variant of David Bowie's "Legends," sung by Depp. In 2020, Depp delivered a front of John Lennon's "Disengagement" with guitarist Jeff Beck and expressed that they would deliver more music together later.

LAWFUL ISSUES

Depp was captured in Vancouver in 1989 for attacking a safety officer after the police were called to end a noisy party at his lodging. Likewise, he was arrested in New York City in 1994 after making huge harm in his room at The Mark Hotel, where he was remaining with Kate Moss, his sweetheart. The charges were dropped against him after he consented to pay US$9,767 in harm. Depp was captured again in 1999 for fighting with paparazzi outside an eatery while feasting in London with Paradis.

In 2012, incapacitated UC Irvine clinical teacher Robin Eckert sued Depp and three security firms, professing to have been gone after by his guardians at a show in Los Angeles in 2011. She was purportedly cuffed and hauled 40 feet across the floor during the episode, bringing about wounds including a disjoined elbow. She contended in court that, as the safety officers' immediate director, Depp neglected to intercede, despite the fact that he didn't partake in the battery. Before the case went preliminary, Depp settled with Eckert for an undisclosed total, as indicated by TMZ.

In April 2015, Depp's significant other, Amber Heard, penetrated Australia's biosecurity regulations when she neglected to proclaim her and Depp's two canines to the traditions when they traveled to Queensland, where he was chipping away at a film. Heard confessed to misrepresenting quarantine records, expressing that she had committed an error because of lack of sleep. She was put on a $1,000 one-month acceptable conduct bond for creating a bogus record; Heard and Depp likewise delivered a video in which they were sorry for their behavior and asked individuals to comply with the biosecurity regulations. The Guardian considered the case the "most prominent crook quarantine case" in Australian history.

In March 2016, Depp cut attaches with his administration organization, The Management Group, and sued them in January 2017 for supposedly inappropriately dealing with his cash and leaving him more than $40 million owing debtors. TMG expressed that Depp was answerable for his monetary botch and countersued him for neglected charges. In a connected suite, Depp additionally sued his legal advisor, Bloom Hergott, in January 2017. The two claims were settled, the previous in 2018 and the last option in 2019.

In 2018, two of Depp's previous guardians sued him for neglected charges and hazardous working circumstances, and the suit was gotten comfortable in 2019. Likewise, in 2018, Depp was sued for supposedly hitting and verbally offending a team part while affected by liquor on the arrangement of City of Lies.

POLITICAL PERSPECTIVES

In November 2016, Depp joined the mission Imprisoned for Art to require the arrival of Ukrainian movie producer Oleg Sentsov, who was being held in authority in Russia.

At the Glastonbury Festival 2017, Depp, reprimanding President Donald Trump, inquired: "When was the last time an entertainer killed a president? I need to explain: I'm not an entertainer. I lie professionally. Notwithstanding, it's been some time and perhaps now is the right time". He added, "I'm not implying anything." The remark was deciphered as a source of perspective for John Wilkes Booth, the entertainer who killed Abraham Lincoln. Shawn Holtzclaw of the Secret Service told CNN they knew about Depp's remark, yet that "for security reasons, we can't examine explicitly nor overall terms the means and techniques for how we play out our defensive obligations." Depp apologized right away after that, saying the comment "didn't emerge as expected, and I planned no noxiousness."

LIQUOR AND MEDICATION USE

Depp has battled with liquor abuse and fixation for quite a bit of his life. He has communicated that he began using drugs by taking his mother's "nerve pills" at 11 years of age, smoking at age 12, and by the age of

14, had used "each kind of meds there were." In a 1997 meeting, Depp recognized past maltreatment of liquor during the shooting of What's Eating Gilbert Grape?. In 2013, Depp proclaimed that he had quit drinking liquor, adding that he "essentially received all that he could receive in return"; Depp additionally said, "I researched wine and spirits completely, and they positively examined me also, and we figured out that we got along wonderfully, yet entirely perhaps excessively well." Concerning separation with long-lasting accomplice Vanessa Paradis, Depp said that he "most certainly won't depend on the beverage to ease things or pad the blow or pad what is happening since that might have been lethal."

As per his ex, Amber Heard, Depp "dove into the profundities of neurosis and savagery in the wake of gorging on medications and liquor" during their connection between 2013 to 2016; in a 2018 Rolling Stone profile of Depp, correspondent Stephen Rodrick composed that he had involved ganja in his presence and portrayed him as "on the other hand amusing, tricky and mixed up"; Depp additionally said that the claim made by his previous business supervisors that he had burned through US$30,000 each month on wine was "annoying" since he had spent "undeniably more" than that sum. During his 2020 slander preliminary, Depp conceded to have been dependent on Roxicodone and liquor as well as utilized different substances, for example, MDMA and cocaine, during his relationship with Heard.

GRANTS AND ACHIEVEMENTS

Johnny Depp's most memorable significant honor was the 'London Film Critics' Circle Award' for 'Entertainer of the Year, which he got in 1995 for his jobs in 'Cassanova DeMarco' and 'Ed Wood.'

The flexible entertainer was granted a privileged 'César,' France's public film grant, in 1999.

In 2008, Depp won a 'Brilliant Globe Award for Best Actor - Motion Picture' for his job in 'Sweeney Todd.' He was additionally named 'Best Villain' at the 'MTV Movie Awards for the job later that year.

From 2011-to 2014, the gifted entertainer has won the People's Choice Awards for Favorite Movie Actor in three events.

He has also gotten various Teen Choice and Kids' Choice honors throughout his profession.

He got the 'MTV Generation Award' in 2012, that same year that 'Guinness World Records' recorded Depp as the most generously compensated entertainer.

TOTAL ASSETS

As per Forbes, Depp's total assets are assessed at $400 million, starting around 2015. His typical compensation each year is roughly $50 million, and his payment for every film midpoint is $20 million. While a piece of his yearly pay comes from speculations, such as his winery, Production Company, and different land property, his main profit comes from his films.

DIFFERENT ENDEAVORS

In 2004, Depp established the film creation organization Infinitum Nihil to foster undertakings where he would act as an entertainer or maker. He fills in as its CEO, while his sister, Christi Dembrowski, fills in as president. The organization's initial two film discharges were The Rum Diary and Hugo.

Depp co-possessed the club The Viper Room in Los Angeles from 1993-to 2003 and the eatery bar Man Ray in Paris. Depp and Douglas Brinkley altered people vocalist Woody Guthrie's original House of Earth, which was distributed in 2013.

Printed in Great Britain
by Amazon